Genre Folktale

MW00896011

Essential Question
What choices are good for us?

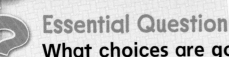

The Weaver of Rugs

A Navajo Folktale

retold by Lana Jones • illustrated by Francisca Marquez

Chapter 1

Searching for Help

Once, the Navajo people did not know how to weave. The winters were very cold where they lived. It was too cold to go out and collect plants or hunt animals. The Navajo became weak from lack of food.

Two women knew they must do something to help their people. They decided to ask the wise ones for help. But wise ones lived in a village far, far away.

The two women set off on their journey. After some time, they became lost in a deep canyon. They sat down on a large rock. "Help!" they called out hopelessly. "Someone help us!"

Suddenly, a tall woman appeared on the cliff high above them. She wove a strong web and threw it down over the women. Then she pulled them all the way up to the top of the cliff.

"I am Spider Woman. Why have you come to annoy me?" a loud voice asked them.

"Our people are cold and hungry," said one of the women. "Can you help them?"

"I will help," said Spider Woman, "but you must do everything I tell you."

Spider Woman wove another strong web. She threw it down into the canyon and over a tree. She tugged at the web and tore the tree out of the ground. She pulled it back up the cliff. Then she broke off four thick branches. She used the branches to make a square frame. After that, she wound her special threads up and down over the frame.

"You will use this loom," she said.

STOP AND CHECK

How did Spider Woman make the loom?

Chapter 2

Learning to Weave

The women were confused.

"You said you would help us," said one.

"How will a loom feed our people?" the other asked.

"Be quiet!" said Spider Woman. "Watch what I am doing."

Spider Woman wove another web. She threw it over some sheep grazing in the canyon below. She pulled them up the cliff. Then she showed the women how to shear the sheep and turn their wool into yarn.

7

"Our people cannot eat yarn," said one of the Navajo women.

"Do you want my help or not?" Spider Woman interrupted.

Then Spider Woman helped the women make dyes from leaves, roots, and berries. She told the women how to dye the yarn. Finally, she taught them to weave the yarn into a rug using the loom.

"You must do the best work you can. Do not be careless and make mistakes," Spider Woman said.

The women worked for days. They wove the yarn in and out of Spider Woman's threads. They became fast, graceful weavers. Still, they could not see how this skill would help their people. The women grew tired of weaving. They began to think Spider Woman would never help them. They got angry and left holes in the rug on purpose.

11

Chapter 3

Finding the Answer

Finally, Spider Woman returned.

"We have done as you asked," one of the Navajo women said.

"Now, we expect you to help our people," said the other one.

"The rug you have woven is imperfect. Go back to your own world," Spider Woman said. "Think about what I have shown you."

The two women were very sad. They went home. They thought that they had failed to help their people. The women wanted to ease the people's problems. They taught the people to weave. They showed the people how to collect wool and turn it into yarn. They showed the people how to dye the yarn many colors and weave it into rugs.

The people wove for their families. They wove for friends. They made more colors from plants. They created many beautiful patterns. The rugs kept them warm. The people wove more rugs than they needed. They traded the extra rugs for food and other goods. At last, health and happiness came into their lives. At last, the two women saw the help Spider Woman had given them.

The women wanted to thank Spider Woman. They cooked a flavorful feast. They carried it all the way to the place they thought was Spider Rock. The luscious aroma of the food drifted all around the canyon.

"Spider Woman!" they shouted. "Spider Woman, where are you?"

They called and called, but Spider Woman never came. After a while, the Navajo people grew famous for their weaving. After a very long time, the two women began to forget about Spider Woman. They wondered if she had ever really existed at all.

STOP AND CHECK

Why did the two women teach the Navajo people to weave?

Respond to Reading

Summarize

Use details in the story to summarize the main events. Your chart may help you.

Details

↓

Point of View

Text Evidence

1. How can you tell this story is a folktale? Genre

2. Reread page 14. How do you think the narrator feels about the Navajo women? Point of View

3. What does the word *hopelessly* on page 3 mean? Root Words

4. Write about how this story would be different if Spider Woman told it. How would she describe the Navajo women? Write About Reading

Compare Texts

Read about making paper mats.

How to Weave Paper Mats

Weaving is a skill that has been around for a very long time. People have woven bags to carry things. People have woven rugs and blankets to keep warm. Not all weaving is difficult. You can weave simple paper mats by yourself.

What You Need:

- Two pieces of colored paper. Each piece should be 12 inches long and 9 inches wide.

- Ruler

- Pencil

- Scissors

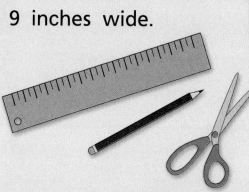

17

What to Do:

1. Fold one sheet of paper in half.

2. Use the ruler to draw a line along an open end of the paper. Make the line 1 inch away from the edge.

3. Make even-spaced cuts up to the line.

4. Cut strips from the second sheet of paper. Each strip should be 9 inches long and 1 inch wide.

5. Unfold the first sheet of paper. Weave one of the strips over and under the cuts in the first sheet of paper.

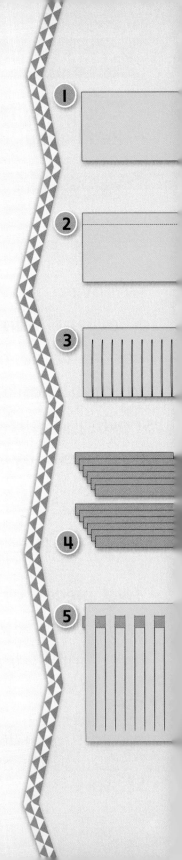

6. Weave the next strip through the paper, swapping the order in which the strip goes over and under.

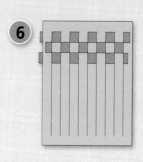

7. Continue weaving the strips through the paper, swapping the order each time. Keep going until you have finished.

Make these mats in a variety of colors. Then you can use them at the dinner table. Enjoy the healthful food you eat on your colorful dinner mats!

Make Connections

How has weaving helped people in the past? Essential Question

The women in the story wove wool into rugs. You wove paper into dinner mats. What other things can people weave? Text to Text

Focus on Genre

Folktales Folktales are stories passed from one person to the next. Folktales are not real. Sometimes, they can have magical events and made-up creatures. Sometimes, folktales can give information about the real world, too.

Read and Find *The Weaver of Rugs* is a folktale with a character that can do magical things. In real life, the Navajo people are very skilled weavers of rugs and other items.

Your Turn

Think of some of the qualities you have. What would happen if they were "larger than life"? Write a story in which you are the hero and you have one or more superpowers.